Everyone was hot.

The children wanted to
go swimming.

Dad said "No!"

# Biff got the paddling pool.

4

Kipper filled it with water.

# Chip pushed Biff in the water.

He grabbed the hose.

They had a water fight.

# Mum got wet.

"Stop it!" said Dad.

# Dad got a bucket of water.

He chased Chip.

# Dad threw the water at Chip.

14

Oh no!

"Sorry!" said Dad.